Mr. Small

by Fay Robinson ❀ illustrated by Janet Drew

Scott Foresman

Editorial Offices: Glenview, Illinois • New York, New York
Sales Offices: Reading, Massachusetts • Duluth, Georgia
Glenview, Illinois • Carrollton, Texas • Menlo Park, California

Mr. Small saw a bird fly by.
"It goes so high!" he said.
"It goes so fast!
It looks like fun!"

"I want to fly," Mr. Small said.
"How does a bird do it?"
He began to pull on his ear.

wing

"I know!" said Mr. Small.
"Birds have wings.
    If I have wings, I can fly."

He worked and worked.
He made some wings.
He pulled them on.

The wings did not work.
He did not fly.

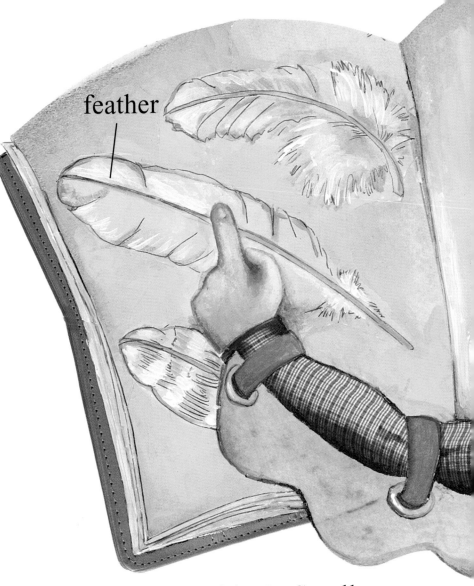

feather

"I know!" said Mr. Small.
"Birds have feathers.
If I have feathers, I can fly."

He worked and worked.
He made some feathers.
He put them on.

The feathers did not work.
He did not fly.

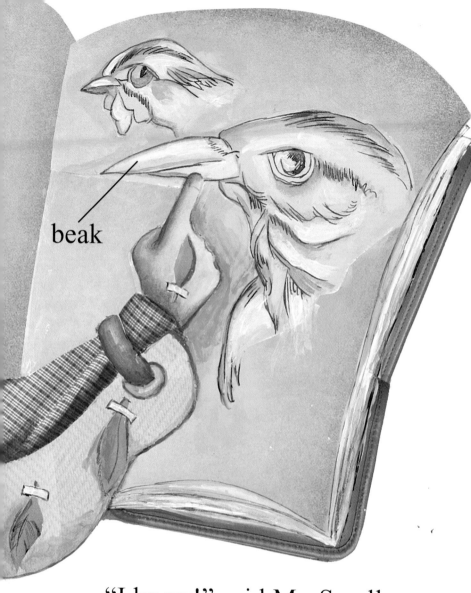

beak

"I know!" said Mr. Small.
"Birds have beaks.
If I have a beak, I can fly."

He worked and worked.
He made a beak.
He pulled it on.

11

The beak did not work.
He did not fly.

"I know!" said Mr. Small.
"Birds have nests.
If I have a nest, I can fly."

He worked and worked.
He made a nest.
He went up to the top of a tree.

He made a friend.

Mr. Small never did fly.
But he was happy anyway.